A PIONEER CHRISTMAS

CELEBRATING IN THE BACKWOODS IN 1841

WRITTEN BY BARBARA GREENWOOD
ILLUSTRATED BY HEATHER COLLINS

KIDS CAN PRESS

To Sheila, for many years of friendship. And to wee Megan and Liam — BG

Kids Can Press acknowledges the financial support of the Ontario Arts Council, the Canada Council for the Arts and the Government of Canada, through the BPIDP, for our publishing activity.

Published in Canada by
Kids Can Press Ltd.
29 Birch Avenue
Toronto, ON M4V 1E2

Published in the U.S. by
Kids Can Press Ltd.
2250 Military Road
Tonawanda, NY 14150

www.kidscanpress.com

Edited by Valerie Wyatt
Designed by Marie Bartholomew
Printed and bound in Hong Kong, China, by Book Art Inc., Toronto

The hardcover edition of this book is smyth sewn casebound.
The paperback edition of this book is limp sewn with a drawn-on cover.

CM 03 0 9 8 7 6 5 4 3 2 1
CM PA 03 0 9 8 7 6 5 4 3 2 1

National Library of Canada Cataloguing in Publication Data

Greenwood, Barbara, [date]
    A pioneer Christmas : celebrating in the backwoods in 1841 / written by Barbara Greenwood ; illustrated by Heather Collins.

Includes index.
ISBN 1-55074-953-6 (bound).   ISBN 1-55074-955-2 (pbk.)

1. Christmas — Canada — History — 19th century — Juvenile literature. 2. Frontier and pioneer life — Canada — Juvenile literature. I. Collins, Heather II. Title.

GT4987.15.G74 2003   j394.2663'0971   C2002-905026-X

Kids Can Press is a *corus*™ Entertainment company

Acknowledgments

I am always pleased to revisit the Robertson family. For the opportunity to share Christmas with them, I am grateful to Valerie Hussey, Rivka Cranley and Brigitte Shapiro.

Many people helped me with background details. Particular thanks go to Marian Bakker for refreshing my memory about the speech patterns of toddlers and for suggesting what Tommy might play with in a farm setting. Thanks, also, to Sheila Fowler for researching Scottish sayings and carols and for her memories of Christmas in Scotland.

Many books provided background on the development of Christmas customs, but the one that pulled it all together was *The World Encyclopedia of Christmas* (McClelland & Stewart, 2000) by Gerry Bowler.

A book is always more than the sum of its parts. For adding their own creative energy to the shaping of this book, my thanks go to: Heather Collins, who once again brought the Robertsons to warm and vibrant life; Marie Bartholomew for her sensitive adaptation of Blair Kerrigan's original design; and my editor, Valerie Wyatt, for the creative brainstorming that always unblocks my path. And, as always, thanks to my husband, Bob, for hours of research and for encouraging me in every project I undertake.

CONTENTS

LOOKING AT CHRISTMAS PAST

Christmas today is a rich mixture of customs from many countries. It all started with the baby in the manger, the shepherds and the visit of the Wise Men. But now we have Santa Claus, a glowing tree with brightly wrapped presents under it, strings of lights, Christmas cards and, on the day itself, a special dinner.

Our Christmas is very different from the Christmas the pioneers celebrated 150 years ago. At first, in their new country, they celebrated Christmas exactly as they had at home. As the years passed, neighbors shared their different customs until Christmas became the celebration we know today.

In this story, the Robertsons, a pioneer family with Scottish roots, await Christmas on their backwoods farm in 1841. All through the fall, as they harvested their crops, Mrs. Robertson set aside the best of everything. Now two fat geese hang ready in the storeroom beside baskets of vegetables and crocks of preserved fruit. To prepare for the special baking, Mr. Robertson has fetched a sack of flour from the mill and Granny has sorted through the raisins from the General Store.

The Robertson children have been busy, too. Meg and Sarah are sewing and knitting small gifts for the family. George and Willy are carving toys. The youngest ones, Lizzie and Tommy, just like children today, feel the excitement in the air.

And they aren't the only ones. All the Robertsons know this will not be an ordinary Christmas. As they go about their preparations, they are waiting for visitors from afar. And, just like the shepherds 2000 years ago, they too are waiting for a very special event.

Ma & Tommy

Meg & Sarah

Granny & Lizzie

Pa

Willy & George

CHRISTMAS
IS COMING!

Sarah picked up an apple and pushed a clove into its shiny, red skin. On the table in front of her were six more apples already studded with cloves. "We're nearly done, Gran. Won't these pomanders smell wonderful all heaped in a bowl on the table?"

"Aye, they'll give the house a good Christmassy smell. Pass over that dish, lassie, and we'll start rolling them."

Sarah pulled the dish of powdered cinnamon and nutmeg closer. The spicy tang mingled with the buttery aroma of shortbread that Ma and Meg were busy baking in the next room.

Was there any smell as wonderful as Christmas?

Sarah deftly punched in the last of the cloves. There. Nice and neat, she congratulated herself. "I think I'll give this pomander to Sophie and Andrew."

"Och, those two! Where can they be?" Granny put down a clove-spiked apple and stared out the window at the snow sifting steadily downward. "All these years, Sarah, with never sight nor sound of family ... To think they're actually on their way. And Andrew—just a lad when we last saw him and here he is married and with a baby coming." She reached for another apple. "Just read your uncle's letter to me again, there's a good lass."

Sarah jumped up to twitch a folded sheet of paper out of the little space under the clock—Ma's safe place for letters. The waxy, red seal had been broken long since, and the letter refolded so many times that it fell open at a touch.

November, 1841, Near Dartmouth

Dear Brother Robert and Family,

A line to let you know we are all well, and we give much thanks for that as there is sickness in the neighborhood. Our big news is that Andrew and Sophie are able to set out at last. Their farm finally sold, so now they have money to buy land near you. We hoped they would be with you long since and are a little worried about Sophie, but trust they will arrive safely before her time ...

Sarah thought about the little crib upstairs — waiting. As soon as the letter arrived, Pa had walled off one corner of the big upstairs room they all shared. Ma and Meg had made up the bed with a feather mattress and Ma's prized red-and-blue quilt. Sarah had padded an apple basket with hay and used soft cloths and knitted shawls to make a warm nest, for the new baby.

"Wouldn't it be wonderful, Gran, if the baby is born on Christmas? Wouldn't it be just the most wonderful Christmas ever?"

"Aye, Sarah, aye. But they have to get here first. If only this snow doesn't blow up into a blizzard. Well ..." she gave a big, gusty sigh, "they'll come in the Lord's good time."

Granny handed Sarah a pomander. "Mind you give this a good dusting, now." They worked in silence, rolling the apples in the spices, then tapping them to shake off the excess. Sarah was tying colored yarn around the last one when she heard a cry from the kitchen.

"Ow! Stop, Tommy! That hurts!"

"Sarah?" It was Ma. "Come and look after this child. This instant!"

Sarah jumped up and ran. Tommy was on his knees next to a pail. Potatoes littered the floor around him, and he was diving into the pail again. Lizzie had one hand pressed to her forehead and the other ready to slap Tommy. Sarah grabbed her wrist.

"Look, Tommy! Let's play Baby Jesus in the Manger." Sarah picked up a tiny, misshapen potato. "Here's a dear little woolly lamb for the shepherds. Come and help me find a camel."

As Sarah nudged Tommy and the pail out of Ma's way, someone banged on the door. Lizzie ran to open it. Willy staggered in, his arms full of firewood. He dropped the bundle, with a great clatter, into the wood box. "Foosh! It's cold out there — cold enough to freeze a bottle of whiskey," he announced, blowing on his hands.

"William Robertson! Wherever did you pick up such an expression?" Ma turned to glare at him.

"That's what Mr. Jamieson at the General Store said to Pa the other day. And it *is* that cold." He rubbed his glowing cheeks and ears.

"Well, don't let me hear you say it again." Ma began sliding cookies onto a plate. "Where's your father and George?"

"Off to the woodlot —" Willy reached a hand toward one of the cookies "— for those big logs they cut last week."

"What! With a storm brewing up?" Ma smacked his hand with the spatula. "If you've nothing better to do, you can finish polishing up the harness bells."

"Aren't we going to make the plum pudding?" Lizzie asked. "You promised we could."

Ma smiled at the little girl. "Yes, Lizzie, I did promise. Why don't you fetch me the bag of raisins. We'll start now."

"Plum pudding!" Lizzie announced in a loud voice and every head turned. If Ma was ready to make the pudding, then Christmas really was coming.

An excited bustle filled the room. Meg chopped suet. Granny and Lizzie sorted through the currants, making a pile of the best ones. Sarah tipped the raisins onto the table. She had just begun to tease out seeds with the point of a knife when a small hand tugged at her apron. "Sweet," Tommy begged. With a quick glance at her mother, Sarah popped a raisin into the little boy's open mouth.

Ma was too busy tasting the batter to notice. "Not quite spicy enough," she decided. "Grate up a little more nutmeg, Meg."

Tommy plunked himself on the floor under the table to march his potato animals up and down, and Sarah slipped into a daydream about the letter. All her life she had heard about the east coast relatives. To think she was actually going to meet a cousin!

"There!" Ma exclaimed, waking Sarah from her dream. "The batter's just right. Time to add everything else." Lizzie poured in the currants. Sarah dumped in her raisins. Then Meg tipped in the shredded suet.

"Stir-up time," Willy shouted and threw down the rag he'd been using to polish the sleigh bells. "Me first?"

"You know the rule—youngest first." Meg scooped Tommy up onto a chair and held his hands around the spoon. "East to west, east to west," she chanted. "Just like the Wise Men going to Bethlehem. Now make a wish."

"More raisins!"

"You don't say it out loud, silly!" Willy hooted. "You'll never get your wish now."

Tommy burst into tears and Lizzie pushed in. "My turn."

The batter was too stiff for her and Ma had to help. Lizzie scrunched up her eyes. "I'm wishing," she announced.

"Well, don't take all day." Willy made a grab for the spoon.

What will I wish for? Sarah wondered. She had planned on wishing for a silver thimble, but ever since the letter had arrived she'd been dithering. Wishing really did work sometimes. The year she'd wished for a pink hair ribbon, her wish had come true. So this time she wouldn't waste it on something silly. This time she had something important to wish for.

When it was her turn, Sarah closed her hands around the wooden

handle of the spoon. East to west. Must do it right. The batter was so thick she had to push hard. But I can't ask for help. Doing it alone is part of the magic.

Once around. Twice around. As she started into the third turn, she pressed her lips together. Not a hint of her wish must escape. Please, she thought, concentrating on the raisins and currants folding in and out of the batter. Please let Cousin Andrew and Sophie get here safely—and let the baby be born in time for Christmas. There, she'd done it.

Finally, when they'd all had a stir, Ma dropped in a small silver coin. "We'll see who's the lucky one this year," she said. Then it was time to tie up the pudding in the linen bag and hang it in the pot of boiling water.

All afternoon the pudding bubbled and steamed, filling the house with succulent smells, but outside a brisk wind was driving hard pellets of snow against the windows. "Just look at that snow," Ma said every so often. "Where *is* your father?"

To take her mind off the rising storm, Sarah carried one of the pomanders upstairs. She ducked behind the quilt that sectioned off the visitors' corner. On the bed sat her apple basket crib. She smoothed out the woolly coverlet. How exciting it would be to have a new baby in the house! If only Andrew and Sophie were here now, safe and snug with us. The pomander was already filling the tiny space with a welcoming scent. I'll just hang it from the bedpost, she thought, reaching up, and by the time they arrive ...

"They're here!" Willy shouted from downstairs. Sarah's heart jumped. At last! She ran to the window. Dimly, through the dense whirl of snow, she saw oxen pulling a sleigh up the lane. Oh! She let out a sigh. Just Pa and George. Then she felt a pang of guilt. Even *they* might get lost in a storm like this. She sent up a small prayer. Thank goodness they're home. And please keep Andrew and Sophie safe this stormy night.

STIR-UP SUNDAY

The ritual of mixing up the plum pudding was the start of Christmas celebrations for the Robertsons and for many pioneer families who had come from Britain. The pudding was such an important part of the Christmas meal that many traditions gathered around it.

Some families made their pudding on the first Sunday of Advent, the day that marked the beginning of the Christmas season. In church that day, one reading from the prayer book began, "Stir up, we beseech Thee, O Lord, the souls of Thy faithful people ..." And so, the day came to be known as Stir-Up Sunday.

As family members took turns stirring, they each made a wish. To make the wish come true, you had to stir from east to west as a reminder of the journey of the three Wise Men. And just as the Wise

Men brought presents to the Baby Jesus, the family added treasures to the pudding — raisins and spices that were expensive and hard to come by in a pioneer community. Last of all, a small silver coin was dropped into the batter to bring good luck to the person who found it on Christmas Day.

After the pudding had been tied up in a linen cloth and boiled, it was stored away for several weeks to let the flavors blend. All these traditions made Stir-Up Sunday an exciting beginning to the family's Christmas preparations.

Making a Pomander

In cities, pomanders were often made with oranges, but people living in backwoods communities made do with apples. Here's how to make a pomander.

You'll need:
- newspapers
- a box of whole cloves
- an apple or orange
- 10 mL (2 tsp.) ground cinnamon
- 10 mL (2 tsp.) ground ginger
- a small paper bag
- 2 pieces of yarn or ribbon, each 60 cm (24 in.) long

1. Spread newspapers on a table to keep it clean. Push the stem of one clove into the apple. Push in a second clove next to the first one. Continue until the apple is completely covered.

2. Put the cinnamon and ginger into the paper bag. Shake well. Put one clove-covered apple into the bag and shake until it is coated with spices. Remove the apple and shake it to get rid of the extra spices.

3. Knot one piece of ribbon around the apple. Knot the second piece around the apple at right angles to the first.

4. Knot two ends to form a loop and tie the other two ends into a bow. Hang the pomander to let it dry and harden. Then use it to scent a closet. Every few months, freshen the smell by shaking the pomander in a bag with more spices.

Winter Games

In the weeks before Christmas, snow blanketed the Robertson's farm, turning the barnyard into a playground. Just like modern children, the Robertsons rode sleds down slippery slopes, made snow forts and threw snowballs. When the ice was thick enough on the river, the boys went skating. The girls didn't because skating was considered unladylike. The older Robertson children sometimes pulled the younger ones on a sled or hitched the dog to the sled and let it do the work. Groups of children joined together for a game of Aunty, Aunty, Over the Shanty. Here's how to play it.

You'll need:
- 4 or more players
- 2 piles of snowballs
- a small building

1. Divide the players into two teams. Each team piles snowballs on their side of the small building.

2. One player is "it" and throws a snowball over the roof, while his team chants "Aunty, Aunty, Over the Shanty."

3. If a player on the opposite side catches the snowball, her team runs around the building to tag the opposing team. Any player tagged joins the other team.

4. The teams return to their own sides, and the second team throws a snowball and chants the rhyme.

5. If nobody catches the snowball, the other team throws a snowball back, calling out the rhyme. The game ends when all players are on one side, or when the group agrees to stop.

To play this game in summer, use one ball and take turns throwing it.

AN UNEXPECTED VISITOR

Sarah was sitting by the front window, knitting, when the sound of sleigh bells made her look out. "It's the Burkholders," she announced. "No, it's Aunt Nettie by herself." She jumped up to open the door.

Lizzie came running. "What did you bring us, Aunt Nettie?"

"Lizzie!" Sarah and Meg turned on their little sister, but Mrs. Burkholder was laughing as she came through the door.

"Nothing for now, *liebchen*. But here's for later."

Lizzie reached for the tin Mrs. Burkholder held out. "Cookie angels! And look, a lamb. And here's a star." Everyone crowded around Lizzie.

"For the Christmas tree," Aunt Nettie said. "No, you have not the tree, like us," she corrected herself. "So for decorating the house."

"And for you, Janet," she turned to Ma and held out a small, linen-wrapped parcel, "some good luck for the coming year."

"Let me see the good luck." Lizzie stood on tiptoe as her mother unwrapped the parcel. "Candles?"

"Special candles. Made with the bayberries my sister sent from Pennsylvania."

"Bayberries!" Granny had hobbled in from the parlor when she heard the babble of voices. "How kind, Nettie. I haven't had a sniff of bayberries for years. Isn't that just the thing to set in the window on Christmas Eve?"

And maybe, Sarah thought, running a finger over the pale green candles, maybe they're just the good luck we need to bring Andrew and Sophie safely through the storms.

PIONEER CHRISTMAS GIFTS

Christmas visitors often brought gifts with them—special baking or practical items such as soap or candles. Nettie Burkholder had used the waxy covering of bayberries to scent her beeswax candles. Since bayberries were scarce, these candles were made only at Christmastime. They were thought to bring good luck.

Gifts were not an important part of a pioneer Christmas, but families often made a few things for the children. Granny knitted warm mitts, Meg made a rag doll for Lizzie, and George and Willy carved toys for Tommy. And this year, Sarah had made a crib for the new baby.

Making a Cup-and-Ball Toy

George whittled a cup-and-ball toy for Willy. You can make one, too.

You'll need:
- a hole punch
- a cardboard cylinder from a toilet paper roll
- string, 40 cm (15 in.) long
- a small, cone-shaped paper cup
- tape
- a hammer and nail
- 2 plastic soft-drink bottle caps

1. Use the hole punch to make a hole in the cardboard cylinder near one edge. Tie one end of the string through the hole.

2. Wedge the paper cup into the end of the cylinder. Tape securely to the cylinder.

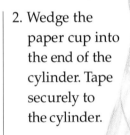

3. Ask an adult to use the hammer and nail to make holes in the centers of both bottle caps.

4. Tape the caps together to make a "ball." Thread the end of the string through the holes and tie it.

5. To play, hold the cylinder and swing the "ball" gently out and up, trying to catch it in the cup. Your skill will improve the more you play.

Making Cookie Decorations

The custom of decorating a tree at Christmas came to North America with German settlers like the Burkholders. Their tree was lit with small candles and hung with gingerbread cookies, called *lebkuchen*, cut into angel, star and animal shapes. Some cookie decorations were soft enough to eat. But this recipe yields a dough that bakes hard as clay and will last for several years.

You'll need:
- 1 L (4 c.) white flour
- 250 mL (1 c.) salt
- 375 mL (1½ c.) water
- a rolling pin
- cookie cutters
- a drinking straw
- acrylic craft paints
- acrylic varnish (optional)
- pieces of colored string, ribbon or yarn

1. Mix the flour and salt in a bowl. Pour in a bit of water, then mix it in with your hands. Continue this way until all the water has been used. Knead the dough for a few minutes until it feels like clay.

2. Dust a little flour onto a table. Roll out the dough to less than 0.5 cm (¼ in.) thick. Use the cookie cutters to cut out shapes.

3. Use the end of the straw to poke a hole near the top of each cookie.

4. Use a spatula to set the cookies on a cookie sheet. Ask an adult to help you put them in an oven preheated to 150°C (300°F). Bake for about 40 minutes. Ask an adult to remove them from the oven.

5. Let the cookies cool completely and then paint them. To keep the colors from running, paint one color, then let it dry. When you are done, paint on a layer of acrylic varnish.

6. Thread ribbon or yarn through the hole and knot it. Hang the ornaments on the Christmas tree.

CHRISTMAS
CAROLING

Sarah sat up straight, her feet flat on the floor of the chilly schoolroom, and opened her mouth to sing with the others. "Doh, ti, la, soh ..."

"High and light, young ladies. And please, gentlemen, no growling." Mr. Taylor walked up and down the rows, beating time. He stopped beside Sarah. Was he listening to Rachel or to her? Sarah's heart skipped a beat as he moved past and leaned over to listen to Meg.

Would he decide tonight? Last week, halfway through a carol they were practicing for the Christmas Frolic, Mr. Taylor had said, "I think we might have a solo for one of these verses."

Choose me! Oh, please, choose me, Sarah had silently begged. At home, she'd been practicing Granny's "Baloo, Lammy" to sing to Sophie and Andrew's new baby. But a lullaby was so soft, and Rachel had such a sweet voice. Would Mr. Taylor choose her instead?

Sarah felt Meg shift sideways and turned in time to see her darting a shy glance down the row of singers. Sarah leaned forward a fraction and caught the bright eyes of their new neighbor, Simon Elliot, seeking out Meg's.

So that's it, Sarah thought. Ma had had a few sharp words to say about Meg's primping in front of the looking glass before they'd set off that evening. Did Ma know why Meg had spent every spare minute this week finishing off a new collar for her dress?

"Quiet, please, ladies and gentlemen." Mr. Taylor tapped his baton on the lectern. "Time to run over our first carol." He struck his tuning fork against the desk and a note quivered in the air.

On the downbeat, Sarah opened her mouth wide and sang in a loud, clear voice, "Deck the halls with boughs of holly ..." Right in the middle of the first fa-la she felt an elbow jab her in the side. She broke off with a small squeak. Meg, still singing, was glaring at her. Sarah glared back. Well! He did say to sing clearly. Then she saw Mr. Taylor raising his eyebrows at her. Hastily she joined in, careful to keep her voice low as she leaned away from Meg's sharp elbow.

All the voices bloomed out into the last, joyous "Fa-la-la-la-la. La, la, la, la."

"Ver-r-ry good." Mr. Taylor was grinning broadly. "That is sure to be the hit of the evening. Well, now. That and 'O Christmas Tree' make two cheery tunes. It would be nice to have a quiet one in between."

"I know one!" The words popped out before Sarah could think. "My Granny's Christmas lullaby."

"Sing it for us," Mr. Taylor invited.

Just the chance she'd wanted! She opened her mouth — and felt her throat go dry. What were the first words? She'd been singing them all week but ... "Meg and I will sing it," she croaked.

She saw Meg staring at her, wide-eyed, and said pleadingly, "Meg?" For a second Meg looked furious, then, with a quick glance around at the waiting faces, she took a deep breath and hummed a starting note. It was all Sarah needed.

"This day to you is born a child ..." Light and high, Sarah thought, light and high, as their voices soared. Then the melody dipped down, down, "... rejoice both heart and mind. Baloo, Lammy," until their voices blended softly on the last mournful note.

For a long moment, there was silence. Sarah swallowed and stared hard at the toes of her boots. She couldn't bear to look at anyone. Then the Singing School broke into wild clapping.

Sarah felt her cheeks go hot. Finally, she dared look up and saw that Meg, too, was blushing furiously. Mr. Taylor had his hand up for silence. "Very nice, young ladies." He sounded surprised. "That might be just the piece for our quiet interlude. I believe ..." he regarded them through narrowed eyes, tapping one finger on the desk "... I believe we'll have a duo for that one."

SINGING SCHOOL

Singing carols at the Christmas Frolic was the highlight of the year for members of the Singing School. This was one of many groups that met over the winter when there were few farm chores to do.

Most communities had at least one person with a good voice and a little musical training who could be coaxed to form a choir. On winter evenings, the singing teacher held classes in a home, school or inn. Because few backwoods homes had pianos or any other musical instruments, the teacher tapped a tuning fork on the desk, then set it down on its stem to give a starting note. But mostly, the group learned to sing by imitating his own strong voice.

This was a social occasion as well as a class. The boys brought the firewood and the girls competed with each other to see who could bring the most attractively decorated candles. For the older girls and boys, it was also an opportunity for flirting and courting. Later in the season, the class would give recitals to raise money to pay the teacher. But performing carols at the Christmas Frolic marked the beginning of their winter activities.

CHRISTMAS CAROLS

Settlers in the backwoods came from many different countries, and at Singing School, they shared songs from home. English settlers brought "Deck the Halls" and many other carols to their new land. German carols such as *"O Tannenbaum"* ("O Christmas Tree") were introduced by German settlers. Sarah and Meg taught the class "Baloo, Lammy," a Scottish carol often sung as a lullaby. Its title means "Hush, Little Lamb."

Baloo, Lammy (Hush, Little Lamb)

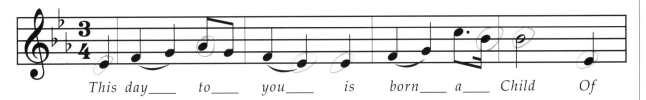

This day___ to___ you___ is born___ a___ Child Of

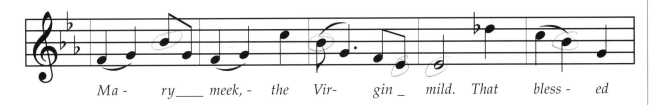

Ma - ry___ meek, - the Vir- gin _ mild. That bless - ed

bairn, ___ so lov - ing and __ kind, Shall now ___ re -

joice ___ both heart ___ and ___ mind. Ba - loo, ___ Lam - my.

O Tannenbaum

O Tannenbaum, O Tannenbaum
Wie treu sind deine Blätter.
Du grünst nicht nur zur Sommerzeit,
Nein, auch im Winter, wenn es schneit,
O Tannenbaum, O Tannenbaum,
Wie treu sind deine Blätter.

O Christmas Tree

O Christmas tree, O Christmas tree,
With faithful leaves unchanging.
Not only green in summer's heat,
But also winter's snow and sleet,
O Christmas tree, O Christmas tree,
With faithful leaves unchanging.

LET THE FESTIVITIES BEGIN

Sarah and Meg pushed their way through the still applauding crowd toward the corner of the room where Ma and Pa were sitting with Granny and the Burkholders.

We did it. We did it! Sarah felt herself grinning, but she couldn't help it. She'd been so nervous. Until the very moment she'd opened her mouth and heard her voice blending with Meg's, she'd been absolutely sure she couldn't.

"Here they are!" Uncle Jacob boomed as they dodged around a

knot of people. "Our singing angels. Were they not angelic, Nettie?"

Aunt Nettie smiled and nodded. "Heavenly!"

"Very nicely done," Ma said primly, bouncing Tommy to keep him from wriggling off her lap. Ma never liked her children to feel too pleased with themselves. "There's always room for improvement" was her motto. But Granny was reaching for Sarah's hand and there were tears in her eyes.

Latecomers were still streaming up the stairs, greeting friends and neighbors as they flowed into the big meeting room. In one corner, Willy and a few other children had started a game of Blind Man's Buff. Sarah was about to join them when the screech of bows on strings made her clap her hands over her ears.

"They're tuning up!" Meg's eyes sparkled. "Is Simon here?" She scanned the room.

"Dancing," Granny said, wistfully. "My old knees won't let me do that anymore. How well I remember ..."

Just then a group of young men came pushing into the room. The last one was Simon Elliot, his arms full of evergreens.

"What a commotion those lads are making," Granny grumbled as she struggled to her feet. "Here, Meggie. Come and help me down the stairs. I'm best off visiting with my friends over the eats."

In the doorway, Simon Elliot had climbed onto a chair and was boosting a ball of evergreens toward a hook in the ceiling.

"I know what you're up to, young man." Granny poked her cane at Simon while the others hooted at him. He jumped down lightly, grinning at Granny, and ducked away from her jabbing stick. Swaying above them was a ball of evergreen branches decorated with a big, red bow.

"Caught you under the kissing ball," Simon announced and gave Granny's cheek a smacking kiss.

"Och, away with ye!" Granny flapped her free hand at them and they ran off laughing. "Kissing ball, indeed," she grumbled. "What a thing to have at a respectable party." Then she saw the look on Meg's face. "Don't you pay any mind to yon great gowk, Meggie. If he had the sense the Lord gave a goose, 'tis you he'd be kissing, not me."

Sarah heard the thump of Granny's cane as she started down the stairs. Then Granny's voice drifted back through a lull in the chatter and bustle. "Still — it did bring back memories."

THE KISSING BALL

Granny knew what everyone at the Christmas Frolic knew — if you were caught under the kissing ball, you'd be soundly kissed.

In the old country, kissing balls were elaborate affairs made from barrel hoops slipped one inside the other in the shape of a ball. The hoops were covered in holly, ivy, boxwood and yew. Around a candle set in the middle hung apples and oranges. Sprigs of mistletoe were suspended beneath. Anyone caught under the mistletoe had to forfeit a kiss. This gave the evergreen ball its name.

Early settlers discovered that holly, ivy and mistletoe didn't grow in their new country. They made kissing balls by tying together branches of local evergreens such as cedar, spruce or pine. Hung by a doorway or in the center of a room, to catch as many guests as possible, the kissing ball added a little extra excitement to the fun of the Christmas season.

THE CHRISTMAS FROLIC

The Christmas Frolic was a community gathering at the local inn. Families like the Robertsons traveled through the dark forest in big ox sleighs kept warm by layers of straw and fur robes. Heated stones wrapped in blankets and tucked under the robes warmed their feet.

At the inn, everyone flocked into the brightly lit hall, stamping snow from their boots. The women headed for the dining room to set out plates of their special holiday food on the long table. Some of the men went into the tavern (the front room of the inn) to play checkers. The young people dashed upstairs to the big meeting room where all the fun would take place.

The second story of the inn was divided into two sections. On one side of the staircase was a hallway leading to several small bedrooms that were rented out to travelers. On the other side was a large room, running the full length of the inn, that was used for neighborhood meetings and parties.

At one end of the long, narrow room was a platform. Here members of the Singing School gathered to perform. When their recital was over, all the chairs were pushed to the sides to make room for dancing.

Most communities had one or two men who could play the fiddle well enough to keep the beat going. Up on the platform, or sometimes perched on a table, a fiddler would tap the time with one foot as he scraped out lively jigs and reels such as "Pop Goes the Weasel" or "The Virginia Reel."

Everyone danced in pioneer times—not just courting couples and husbands and wives, but also grandmothers with their grandsons, and brothers with their sisters. They lined up facing each other, someone offered to "call off" the dance and to shouts of "Face your partner" and "Grand promenade all," the fun began.

Blind Man's Buff

At the Christmas Frolic, the younger children gathered to play games. A great favorite was Blind Man's Buff (named for the "buffet" or light tap the other players gave the "blind" man).

You'll need:
• 4 or more players
• a scarf

1. Choose one player to be the Blind Man. Tie a scarf over the Blind Man's eyes, then have two players take hold of his arms and gently spin him around three times.

2. All the players dart around the Blind Man, touching him or calling to him. The Blind Man tries to catch one of them. When he does, he has to guess the identity of his captive. If he does, the captured player becomes the new Blind Man.

CHRISTMAS GARLANDS

"Two days to go! Two days to go!" Lizzie chanted. She was skipping around the table where Sarah and Meg sat threading popcorn onto long strings.

Another one done, Sarah thought, tying a final knot in the end of her string. She pictured the strings of white popcorn intertwined with dark red cranberries, all looped over the fresh green boughs. The garlands were going to look wonderful this year.

Lizzie's chant grew louder. Meg looked up. "Hush, Lizzie—you'll wake Tommy."

Sarah put out an arm to stop the little girl. "Why don't you be our lookout, Lizzie? You can watch out the parlor window for Pa and the boys. Remember ..." she put a finger to her lips. "Quiet as a mouse."

Lizzie thought for a moment, eyes narrowed, then nodded and tiptoed into the parlor. At last the house was silent, except for the odd crackle from the fire and the soft drone of Granny's snores.

Sarah threaded her needle again. Wordlessly, the sisters worked their way through the popcorn. With Lizzie out of the way, they'd be finished long before Pa and the boys got back with the cedar boughs.

"I see them!" Lizzie shrieked and ran to fling the door open, letting in a swoosh of cold air. Sarah heard Granny mumbling in her bedroom. Tommy gave a thin, waking-up cry, then Ma's footsteps sounded on the stairs.

Lizzie danced out of the way as Willy burst into the room and dumped his load of greenery on the floor. At last, Sarah thought, gathering up a fragrant armful. At last.

By suppertime, the house was festooned with garlands. They were strung across the window tops, draped over the mantelpiece and mounded on top of the dish dresser.

"What about Aunt Nettie's cookies?" Lizzie asked, looking up from playing potato animals with Tommy.

"We'll tie those on after supper," Ma promised.

Sarah was setting the table. "This time tomorrow, Sophie and Andrew will be here."

"Now don't get your hopes up, lassie," was Granny's predictable reply.

"But it's the last coach before Christmas. It has to be tomorrow." Or, Sarah thought wistfully, my wish won't come true.

"Aye, but ye mind well, hinny, there's nothing certain about December weather. I've told ye what happened to us when we were caught by a blizzard all those years ago ..."

How often, Sarah wondered, had she heard Granny's story about their own family's trip from the east coast when the stagecoach stuck fast in a snowdrift.

"... And me breaking a path, wading knee-high through the snow with poor, wee Georgie struggling behind. Your mother had you bundled in her shawl and Meggie clinging to her skirts. It's a wonder we ever reached that inn!"

Meg looked up from slicing bread. "Let's hope the snow keeps off. How would Sophie ever manage snowdrifts — with the baby so near to being born?"

Ma and Granny exchanged a glance that made Sarah's heart thump. Please, she prayed, as she set out the last of the dishes. Please let them be on the next coach.

WINTER TRAVEL

The Robertsons had good reason to worry about Andrew and Sophie. Travel in pioneer times was difficult, dangerous and slow. Most roads were little more than rutted paths. In rainy weather, stagecoach wheels bogged down in the mud, leaving passengers stranded.

Winter made travel easier in some ways but harder in others. The mud froze, and packed snow "paved" the roads so that stagecoaches could skim along on sled runners. But blizzards could trap passengers for days in crowded inns, and drifting snow could block the way, forcing passengers to walk to the next inn or help dig out the road.

Stagecoaches carried four or six passengers. Their luggage was strapped to the roof or onto a carrier at the back. Two drivers sat on an open seat in front. Inside, the passengers huddled together, cramped, cold and miserable.

The coaches made regular stops at inns spaced about 25 km (15 mi.) apart. An inn that stood halfway between two settlements was often called a Halfway House. As the stagecoach approached an inn, the driver sounded his horn to alert the ostlers (workers who tended the horses) to trot out a fresh team. After being crammed into the freezing coach with only blankets and the often foul-smelling body heat of other passengers for warmth, everyone was grateful for a brief stop. It gave passengers a few minutes to stretch their legs and catch a breath of fresh air or have a hot drink in the inn. Around noon, the stop was long enough for a meal.

By evening, passengers were eager to stop for the day. At the inn they found warmth in front of a roaring fire and a hot meal. Everyone sat down to supper at one long table, then it was off to bed to be ready for a dawn start.

Families or women traveling alone could sometimes rent a small room for the night, but single men were allotted space in a bed shared with two or three others. If the inn was full, some passengers slept on the floor of the big upstairs meeting room. Many preferred the hard floor to beds where the sheets were seldom changed, and fleas and bedbugs made a sound sleep impossible.

How would Andrew and Sophie — with a baby on the way — stand such a journey, the Robertsons worried. How relieved everyone would be to have them safe and snug in their own comfortable house.

DECORATING THE HOUSE FOR CHRISTMAS

"It was always holly and ivy back home," Granny said as Sarah and Meg snipped and sorted the greenery for the garlands. "How those holly berries brightened up our wee croft."

The Robertsons and their pioneer neighbors used whatever they could find in forest or field to carry on the traditions they'd brought with them from the old country. They used cranberries in place of holly berries and spruce or cedar boughs for their garlands. Some years, they just gathered evergreen boughs into bunches and tied them with ribbon.

Making a Garland

Garden nurseries and grocery stores often have boughs at Christmastime. Or ask an adult to help you cut some evergreen boughs. Cedar works best.

You'll need:
- evergreen boughs about 50 cm (20 in.) long
- heavy string or cord the length you want to make your garland
- thin wire

1. Place a row of boughs along the length of the string, and bind them on with the wire. Look for thinly covered sections. Add more boughs to make the garland full and dense.

2. Decorate your garland by winding strings of popcorn and cranberries around it or by tying on cookies, cones, small colored ornaments or ribbons.

3. Use the garland to decorate a mantel, table or cabinet.

CHRISTMAS EVE

"Hand me up another one, Lizzie." Sarah was perched on a chair, stretching to tie one of Aunt Nettie's cookies onto the garland draped over the parlor window. Four more already hung among the greenery. After supper, Ma had said, yes, Sarah and Lizzie could finish decorating the garlands. It would give Lizzie something to do, Sarah had pointed out. But she had to admit — she, too, was glad of a distraction.

Without looking, she reached for the next cookie, but nothing came. She glanced down to find Lizzie staring off into space. "Maybe ..." Lizzie intoned, her voice whispery and mysterious, "maybe Sophie and Andrew won't ever come. Maybe they're lost. Frozen in the forest ..."

"Lizzie! Don't you let Ma hear you talking like that." Sarah gave a quick look toward the door to the kitchen. No happy chattering. Just a grim silence broken by the occasional clattering of pans.

How disappointed they'd felt yesterday when Pa and George returned from the village alone. They'd been so sure that Andrew and Sophie would be on the stagecoach. No passengers at the Halfway House, Pa reported. They'd even waited while Mr. Jamieson at the General Store sorted through the mail pouch, but he'd found no letter to explain the delay. "They've been storm-stayed," Pa had said a little too heartily. "They're sure to be safe at an inn along the way."

After that, Ma's face had set in a tight, far-off look. And Granny had taken to staring into the fire and rocking herself with fierce determination, as though, by sheer willpower, she might spur them on.

Just then a cookie slid from Lizzie's hand and smashed on the floor. With an exasperated "Tch," Sarah hopped down. She was scooping the last few crumbs into her apron pocket when Willy called, "It's time."

Sarah's spirits lifted. "Come on, Lizzie." She held out her hand.

In the kitchen, George was gathering chairs and stools in a circle around the fire. Meg scooped up Tommy. "Give the wee lamb to me." Granny reached out from her rocker.

Sarah pulled the high-backed settle closer to the fire so that she and Lizzie could snuggle together in the warmth, then moved over to make room for Willy.

"Well now," Pa said in a voice that tried hard to sound cheerful. "Let's start by remembering those far away."

Sarah gazed into the fire. For years, they had lived too far back in the bush to get to church on Christmas Day, but she treasured their own way of celebrating. Pa always started with a roll call, as though by naming their

distant family he could draw them into the circle around the fire. "And this year," Pa finished, "our prayers are with Andrew and Sophie. May they be safe and warm wherever they find themselves this holy night."

In Pa's lap lay the family Bible, the same Bible that had traveled all the way from the old world to the new world to this room. As he opened it now, Sarah waited for the words they knew so well.

"And there were in the same country shepherds, abiding in the field, keeping watch over their flocks by night." Sarah looked round the circle as her father's voice flowed over them. Even Tommy, sucking his thumb, and Meg and George sitting, almost grown up, on their own separate chairs were caught up in the old, old story.

"And this shall be a sign unto you: Ye shall find the babe wrapped in swaddling clothes, lying in a manger ..." Sarah thought of the homemade cradle waiting upstairs — so much cozier than a manger.

"And when they had returned, they made known abroad all they had heard concerning this child. And all they that heard it wondered at these things that were told them by the shepherds." Pa closed the Bible, and from around the circle came satisfied sighs. They could, every one of them, Sarah knew, have recited the whole story of Jesus's birth by heart, but there was something satisfying about sitting together listening to Pa reading to them by firelight.

"A little music," Pa said. "Meg, why don't you and Sarah give us Granny's lullaby?"

As the last notes of "Baloo, Lammy" died away, Ma looked at a yawning Tommy and said, "I think we'll have the candle now." She had put one of Aunt Nettie's special bayberry candles in a tin holder on the table. Pa leaned into the fireplace to light a wooden splint from the embers. Sarah thought with longing of the time when Pa had handed the glowing splint to her, but two years ago she'd given up her place to Willy, and now it was his turn to give way to Lizzie.

Pa handed the splint to the little girl. She held it to the bayberry candle and waited until the wick caught and the light blossomed. Then she carefully carried the candle to the window ledge beside the front door.

"Welcome, strangers," Ma said.

"Welcome, Christ Child," Pa said.

"Welcome, Christmas," they all said together.

Quiet fell over them. Sarah looked around the circle and knew they all shared her prayer as they watched the candlelight reach out into the darkness. Keep our travelers safe.

Then Ma shook herself and said briskly, "Bed for little ones."

Meg had just gathered Tommy out of Granny's arms when Willy sat bolt upright. "What's that?" They all froze. A faraway sound grew louder. "Sleigh bells!"

Pa flung open the door to jingling bells and a voice shouting, *"Whoa! Stehen Sie!"*

The rush to the door was blocked by Pa who called, "Jacob! What are you doing out at this hour of a Christmas Eve?"

Sarah peered through the glass. Could it be? She saw a dark figure climbing out of the sleigh, a bundle being handed down and then another figure descending.

"Is it them? Is it them?" Lizzie poked her head between Pa and the doorframe.

Uncle Jacob's voice boomed, "How's this for a Christmas present? Just a little something I found at the General Store."

Then Pa was back in the room. A young man followed him through the doorway. Sarah could see that he was as tall as Pa and had the same twinkly eyes. One arm was wrapped protectively around a young woman and the bundle she cradled in her arms.

"Is that our Andrew?" Granny hobbled across the room, her stick thumping. "Oh, thank the Lord you're safe." And at the same time, Ma cried, "Mercy! The dear wee bairn!"

"Meet Douglas John." Andrew was all grins as they crowded around to gaze at the sleeping baby. "He came early, so we had to spend close on a fortnight at an inn. This morning a farmer on his way to the mill offered us a ride as far as your village. Then we met Mr. Burkholder. And thanks to him, we're here."

"Come sit by the fire and warm yourself." Ma had recovered from her surprise. "Meg, put the kettle on."

Later that evening, with everyone else laughing and chattering around the table, Sarah took a candle and tiptoed into Granny's bedroom. The baby lay nestled in the basket. She gazed at him with delight. The candle's glow lit up the tiny face, picking out dark lashes resting on ruddy cheeks. His face puckered and he gave a little mew of protest.

Sarah leaned closer. "This day to you is born a child ..." she sang, almost in a whisper "... Baloo, Lammy." The baby's mouth opened in a huge yawn, then closed with little contented, sucking sounds. One tiny hand curled around her finger. She felt as though it had squeezed her heart.

"Douglas John," she whispered. "My Christmas wish come true."

CHRISTMAS DAY

In pioneer times, Christmas Day was not a day of lavish celebration as it often is today. In some homes, usually those close to a town, the children might find stockings they'd hung at the end of their beds filled with nuts, candies and oranges (a once-a-year treat). But farm children usually started the day with chores.

Later in the morning, the women prepared a special dinner of roast goose (fattened all fall especially for this day) and vegetables — boiled potatoes, carrots and squash. Dinner was served at noon, followed by the long-awaited treat — the steaming plum pudding with its hidden silver coin. Apples and nuts finished the meal.

After dinner, the father of the household distributed the small gifts that had been tucked into the garlands or, in German homes, hung on the Christmas tree.

In the afternoon, while the adults rested after the heavy meal, the children went outside to play.

The day ended quietly, with tired children snacking on the remains of Christmas dinner before heading off to bed.

CHRISTMAS THEN AND NOW

Early settlers in North America brought their Christmas traditions with them. The Germans brought evergreen trees indoors and decorated them with angel and star cookies. The Irish set a special candle in the window to welcome the Christ Child, and the English boiled a spicy plum pudding for Christmas dinner. At first, each group followed its own customs. But gradually, as they shared ideas, a new way of celebrating Christmas developed.

Many of the Christmas traditions we cherish today began to develop in the mid-1800s with the publication of Charles Dickens's *A Christmas Carol* and Clement Moore's "A Visit from St. Nicholas."

Clement Moore lived in New York State, where Dutch settlers began each year's Christmas celebrations with the arrival of Sinter Klaas, a stern figure who rewarded good children with gifts but punished bad children. English settlers often welcomed the arrival of another Christmas visitor, St.

Nicholas, also known as Father Christmas. In 1824 Clement Moore combined these traditions in "A Visit from St. Nicholas," which begins, " 'Twas the night before Christmas, when all through the house, not a creature was stirring, not even a mouse." Even though settlers from many backgrounds already gave small gifts to their children at Christmas, this poem made more widespread the idea of children hanging stockings in the hope of receiving presents from a mysterious visitor.

The idea that Christmas should be a time of joyous family celebration grew even stronger with the publication in 1843 of Charles Dickens's *A Christmas Carol*. This story contrasted the dreary, selfish life of rich Ebenezer Scrooge, all alone on Christmas Eve, with the happy family life of the Cratchits. Even though they are too poor to buy presents and a lavish dinner, the Cratchits show by their love and concern for each other what Dickens felt was the true spirit of Christmas. This popular story did much to shape the way people celebrate Christmas.

Around 1850, people began to blend Christmas customs from various backgrounds and earlier times. The German tradition of decorating an evergreen tree was soon followed everywhere. Putting candles in windows had been a tradition for many pioneers, particularly for the Irish who also made small manger scenes to retell the story of the Baby Jesus. By the end of the 19th century, many new carols had been written. Christmas cards to send greetings to faraway friends became popular in 1846 when the mail service had become both efficient and inexpensive.

In the 19th century, Christmas was not a holiday from work. Just like Ebenezer Scrooge in *A Christmas Carol*, many employers expected their employees to work whether it was Christmas or not. Gradually, more and more businesses closed on December 25th. Today Christmas is recognized as a holiday all over North America and in many other parts of the world.

Now, at the beginning of the 21st century, we are so used to the rich blend of Christmas customs that few of us even think about where or how these cherished traditions began. Like the Robertsons, we are content to enjoy the warmth and closeness that Christmas brings.

INDEX